The Story Of AREA 51

by Noah Leatherland

Roar! Books, an imprint of Bearport Publishing by FlutterBee

Credits
Cover and title page, © Zachary Byer/Shutterstock and © Matteo/Adobe Stock and © Pablo Caridad/Shutterstock; 4, © Anna Kucherova/Adobe Stock; 5, © Pornpimon Ainkaew/Shutterstock; 6, © Yuri A/Shutterstock; 6–7, © Dylan.King/Shutterstock; 7, © James Phelps JR/Adobe Stock; 8TR, © Zack Frank/Adobe Stock; 8M, © Andriy Blokhin/Shutterstock; 9, © Doc Searls/Wikimedia; 10, © Artem Sokolov/Shutterstock; 11, © Public Domain/Wikimedia; 12, © U.S. Air Force/Wikimedia; 12–13, © NASA/Wikimedia; 14, © Vytautas Kielaitis/Shutterstock; 14—15, © Raggedstone/Shutterstock; 16, © Zack Frank/Shutterstock; 17T, © Chronicle/Alamy Stock Photo; 17BL, © Chroma Collection/Alamy Stock Photo; 17BR, © UPI/Wikimedia; 18–19, © Eric Draper/AP Photo; 19M, © Fort Worth Star-Telegram/Wikimedia; 19BR, © "Roswell Daily Record"/Wikimedia; 20ML, © George Stock/Wikimedia; 20–21, © Library of Congress; 21, © Steve Jurvetson/Wikimedia; 22–23, © ktsdesign/Shutterstock; 23, © Raggedstone/Shutterstock; 24, © CIA; 25, © Francesco Sgura/Shutterstock; 26, © Trevor Bexon/Shutterstock; 26BR, © missisya/Adobe Stock; 27, © clayton harrison/Shutterstock; 28, © Nebs/Shutterstock; 28–29, © melhijad/Shutterstock; 30, © cody traxler/Shutterstock; 31, © Matteo/Adobe Stock

Bearport Publishing Company Product Development Team
Kayla Eggert, Theresa Emminizer, Kim Jones, Allison Juda, Cole Nelson, Naomi Reich, Steve Scheluchin, Tiana Tran

Library of Congress Cataloging-in-Publication Data is available at www.loc.gov or upon request from the publisher.

ISBN: 979-8-89577-840-1 (hardcover)
ISBN: 979-8-89577-848-7 (ebook)

For more information, write to Bearport Publishing, 3500 American Blvd W, Suite 150, Bloomington, MN 55431. Printed in the United States of America.

CONTENTS

HISTORY'S MYSTERIES

Most stories have a beginning and an end. However, some of them leave behind more questions than answers.

These tales have missing information or unlikely endings.

People have tried to solve famous mysteries for many years. Despite their efforts, parts of some of these stories remain unexplained.

Are you ready to explore a mystery?

THE MYSTERY OF AREA 51

Space is so big that we can never hope to explore it all. This has led some to wonder if humans aren't alone in the universe.

Do **aliens** exist? Many people think they do. Some believe they may have already come to Earth.

If this is the case, where are they? Why have we not seen them?

There may be some answers to these questions inside Area 51.

BEFORE THE MYSTERY

The story of Area 51 begins in the small town of Rachel, Nevada.

A salt flat

In the 1860s, silver and lead were found around a nearby **salt flat** called Groom Lake. People came to mine these valuable metals from the ground.

However, miners weren't the only ones interested in the dry lake bed. The U.S. military had their eyes on Groom Lake, too.

Soon, miners had to share the region. The military wanted to use it for an even bigger project.

THE SECRETS BEGIN

After World War II (1939–1945), the U.S. military needed a base to test new airplanes. They wanted somewhere private and hidden.

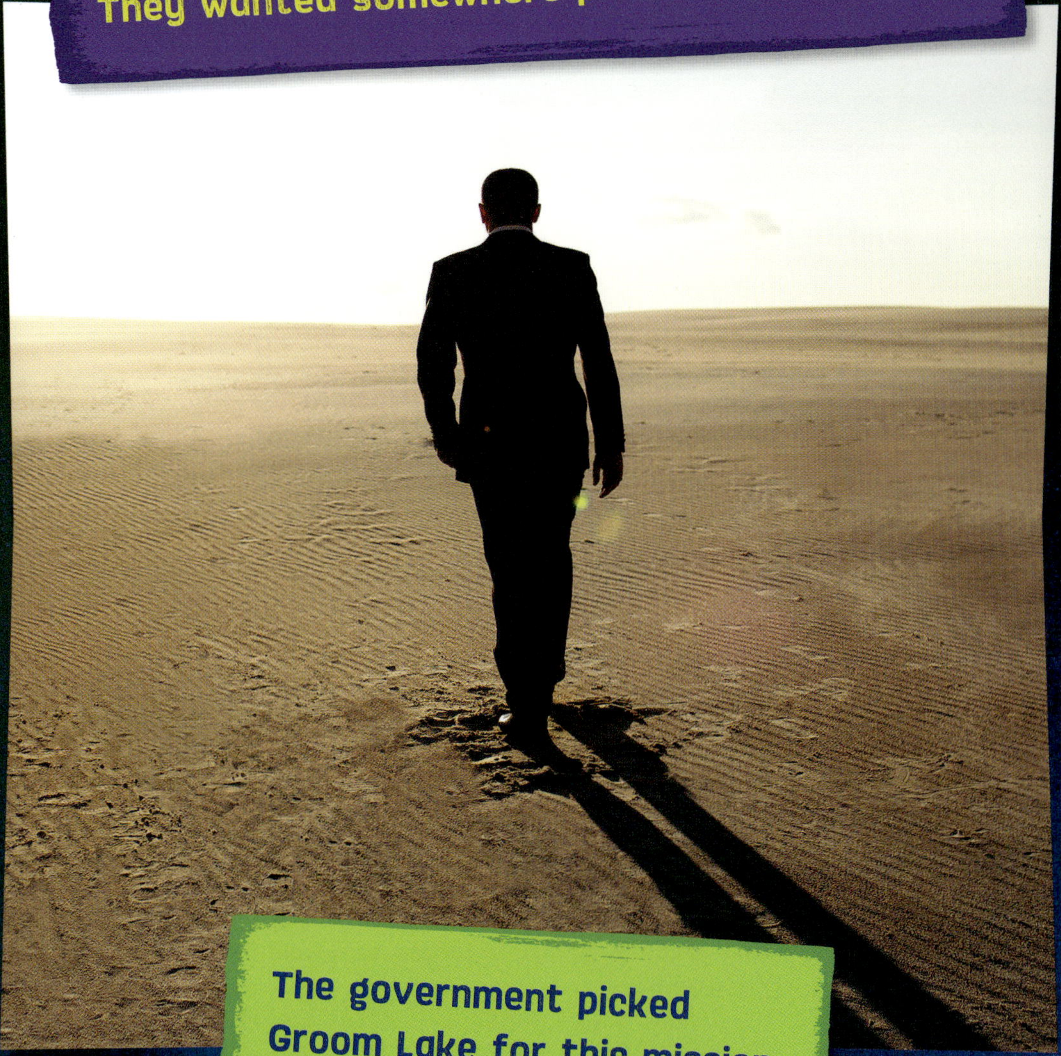

The government picked Groom Lake for this mission.

Groom Lake is in the middle of nowhere. It is surrounded by mountains. This can keep things hidden.

An image of the area taken from above

The flat ground near the lake bed is good for landing planes.

HIDDEN PROJECTS

The government built Area 51. Shortly after, they started a project. The U.S. government wanted to keep an eye on other countries. They were afraid of dangerous weapons.

In 1955, a team of **engineers** went to Area 51. Together, they built the famous U-2 spy plane.

The U-2 could fly above 70,000 feet (21,300 m) high. That was higher than any other plane at the time!

Being so high up in the air made the U-2 hard for **satellites** to spot. This helped the plane secretly gather information about other countries.

LIGHTS IN THE SKY

At first, nobody knew about the U-2 plane. But people living near Area 51 knew the government was up to something.

People around Rachel began spotting strange things in the sky.

These came to be known as unidentified flying objects, or UFOs. The term went on to be used for anything flying through the air that cannot be explained.

As more UFOs made the news, people became curious. What were they? Why were they near Area 51?

FLYING SAUCERS

On June 24th, 1947, Kenneth Arnold had a firsthand experience with a UFO. He was flying a plane. As he came near Mount Rainier in Washington, Kenneth saw a bright flash of light.

Mount Rainier

At first, Kenneth thought it was a military plane. But then, even more flashes appeared.

Kenneth said he saw nine round and shiny objects in the sky. He said they moved like saucers skipping on water. This is how the term flying saucer was born.

Kenneth Arnold

PAGE 2 THE CHICAGO UN, THURSDAY, JUNE 26, 1947

In These United States

Supersonic Flying Saucers Sighted by Idaho Pilot

Speed Estimated at 1,200 Miles an Hour When Seen 10,000 Feet Up Near Mt. Rainier

PENDLETON, Ore., June 25.—
NINE bright, saucer-like objects flying at "incredible" speed at 10,000 feet altitude were reported here today by Kenneth Arnold, Boise (Idaho), pilot, who said he could not hazard a guess as to what they were.
Arnold, a U.S. Forest Service employee searching for a missing

CRASH LANDING

Shortly after Kenneth's report, Mac Brazel found a shiny fabric object. It had crashed on his ranch in Roswell, New Mexico.

Roswell, New Mexico

On July 7th, 1947, Mac took the **debris** to the sheriff. It was then passed along to the nearby army base.

On July 8th, the army base announced that the debris was part of a flying disc. But the next day, they changed their story.

The U.S. military claimed it was a weather balloon. However, Mac did not believe them.

PROJECT BLUE BOOK

Stories of UFOs stacked up. The U.S. government started looking into them in 1947. This was known as Project Blue Book.

UFOs spotted in 1952

The government collected 12,618 reports of UFO sightings. All but 701 of these were explained.

PROJECT

BLUE BOOK

1 FEBRUARY 1966

But before the last of the sightings could be solved, Project Blue Book was shut down. A report from the University of Colorado concluded that there was no **evidence** of the UFOs being alien spacecraft or anything dangerous.

CLAIMS

In 1989, a man who claimed to have worked in Area 51 wanted to share what he knew. He told his stories to a news station in Las Vegas, Nevada.

The man said he worked in a secret building called S-4. His job involved working on alien spaceships.

During the job, the man said he saw actual aliens in Area 51.

His claims were soon proven false. However, this caught lots of people's attention. What was really inside the secret base?

THE SECRETS ARE OUT!

Area 51 documents were **classified** for years. Only a few people were allowed to read these top secret papers.

Declassified in Part - Sanitized Copy Approved for Release 2014/05/08 : CIA-RDP81B00879R001000120175-9

OXC 6112
Copy 5 of 5

10 December 1963

MEMORANDUM FOR THE RECORD

SUBJECT: Report on Trip to Area 51 During Period 2 - 6 December 63

1. Primary purpose of trip was recurrency in F-101 and familiarization front seat ride in A-12. One flight was made in each aircraft with satisfactory results. Basic comment on A-12 is that seat is very uncomfortable, even for one-and-a-half hours, and aircraft is basically an instrument aircraft.

2. I attended a briefing given by [redacted] on Exercise Delta. Comments of this meeting are as follows: 50X1

a. There is a serious timing problem on programming the slit openings for packages A and A1. Solution for present exercise: The package representatives will prepare the slit openings in consonance with [redacted] and the planning staff at Area 51. The possibility exists that these openings could be programmed into our computer, which will give us the option of not disclosing the overflight route to the package representatives. 50X1

b. Destruct cans: No firm policy is available to Area 51 on use of maps or let-down plates. This item will be incorporated in the critique.

c. Problem of loading more than one type package at a time: Limited hanger space at present time is deciding factor, but can be solved by staggering aircraft during exercise. Note: One aircraft will be loaded with Type 1 and one aircraft loaded with Type 1A.

d. Colonel Byerly of Beale Air Force Base would like to attend the critique; undecided at present time as to whether to invite him.

e. Subject of "take" procedures and what is needed after mission from Area 51 is undetermined at this time. Exercise will preclude "take" procedures.

f. Flight of A-12: I have advised [redacted] that he may fly A-12 on local training mission if it does not interfere with Exercise Delta. 50X1

Declassified in Part - Sanitized Copy Approved for Release 2014/05/08 : CIA-RDP81B00879R001000120175-9

Declassified in Part - Sanitized Copy Approved for Release 2014/05/08 : CIA-RDP81B00879R001000120175-9

But that changed in 2013. Some documents about the base became open to the public.

The documents had details about secret projects. Many were about spy planes, such as the U-2.

None of the documents mentioned aliens. However, some documents are still classified. . . .

TODAY

Today, Area 51 is still a military base. The work that goes on inside the base remains top secret. This makes people curious.

STOP

Some tourists come with the idea of exploring Area 51. But they can never make it past security.

The base has 24-hour **surveillance**. There are security officers watching at all times. They keep visitors from entering Area 51.

However, tourists still have plenty of things to do. There are alien-themed shops, restaurants, and hotels near the base. Many people come visit to explore the area and celebrate stories of aliens.

FACT OR FICTION?

With so many questions surrounding Area 51, it's hard to tell what is real and what is fake. What are people asking?

Were any of the UFOs really alien spacecraft? There is no evidence to support this.

What do Area 51 workers actually do? They mainly work on military aircraft.

A lot of claims about Area 51 are not true. However, this is just one of many military bases. There are other places that have their own secrets.

Who knows what might be out there?

THE TRUTH IS OUT THERE!

There are plenty more clues we might yet uncover to solve the mysteries of Area 51. One day, we might get a step closer to the truth.

It is fun to read about mysteries and wonder about what might have happened. What would you like to explore next?

GLOSSARY

aliens beings from another world

classified kept secret or not given to the general public

debris broken pieces of something

engineers people who are trained to design and build machines

evidence information and facts that can be used to prove whether something is true

salt flat a flat area covered in salt that is left after saltwater evaporated

satellites spacecraft placed in orbit that are able to send signals back to Earth

surveillance a close watch kept over someone or something

Index

Read More

Deniston, Natalie. *Area 51 (Do You Believe?).* Minneapolis: Jump!, Inc., 2025.

Redshaw, Hermione. *The Attack of the Aliens (Supernatural Survivor).* Minneapolis: Bearport Publishing Company, 2024.

Walker, Tracy Sue. *34 Amazing Facts About Aliens (Unbelievable!).* Minneapolis: Lerner Publications, 2026.

Learn More Online

1. Go to **FactSurfer.com** or scan the QR code below.
2. Enter "**Area 51 Story**" into the search box.
3. Click on the cover of this book to see a list of websites.